DUDLEY SCHOOLS
LIBRARY SERVICE

KU-368-418

Schools Library and Information Services
S00000729412

World of Farming

# Plants on a Farm

Nancy Dickmann

**www.raintreepublishers.co.uk**
Visit our website to find out
more information about
Raintree books.

**To order:**
☎ Phone 0845 6044371
▤ Fax +44 (0) 1865 312263
▣ Email myorders@raintreepublishers.co.uk

Customers from outside the UK please telephone +44 1865 312262

Raintree is an imprint of Capstone Global Library Limited, a company incorporated in England and Wales having its registered office at 7 Pilgrim Street, London, EC4V 6LB – Registered company number: 6695582

Text © Capstone Global Library Limited 2011
First published in hardback in 2011
The moral rights of the proprietor have been asserted.

All rights reserved. No part of this publication may be reproduced in any form or by any means (including photocopying or storing it in any medium by electronic means and whether or not transiently or incidentally to some other use of this publication) without the written permission of the copyright owner, except in accordance with the provisions of the Copyright, Designs and Patents Act 1988 or under the terms of a licence issued by the Copyright Licensing Agency, Saffron House, 6–10 Kirby Street, London EC1N 8TS (www.cla.co.uk). Applications for the copyright owner's written permission should be addressed to the publisher.

Edited by Siân Smith, Nancy Dickmann, and Rebecca Rissman
Designed by Joanna Hinton-Malivoire
Picture research by Mica Brancic
Production by Victoria Fitzgerald
Originated by Capstone Global Library Ltd
Printed and bound in China by South China Printing Company Ltd

ISBN 978 0 431 19557 5
15 14 13 12 11 10
10 9 8 7 6 5 4 3 2 1

**British Library Cataloguing in Publication Data**
Dickmann, Nancy.
  Plants on a farm. -- (World of farming)
  1. Crops--Pictorial works--Juvenile literature. 2. Farm life--Pictorial works--Juvenile literature.
  I. Title II. Series
  633-dc22

**Acknowledgements**
We would like to thank the following for permission to reproduce photographs: FLPA p.4 (Wayne Hutchinson); Photolibrary pp.5 (Superstock/ Penny Adams), 6 (All Canada Photos/Peter Carroll), **7 main** (Joan Pollock), 8 (imagebroker.net/Florian Kopp), 9 (age fotostock/Javier Marina), 10 (F1 Online/Photo Thomas Gruener), 11 (fStop/Ragnar Schmuck), 12 (Garden Picture Library/Claire Higgins), 13 (Index Stock Imagery/Inga Spence), 14 (Cusp/Stock Photos/Bruce Peebles), 16 (age fotostock/Martin Rugner), 18 (Chad Ehlers), 19 (Tips Italia/Massimo Fornaciari), 20 (Index Stock Imagery/ Lynn Stone), 21 (Blend Images/Karin Dreyer), 22 (Tips Italia/Massimo Fornaciari ), **23 top** (Index Stock Imagery/Lynn Stone); Shutterstock pp.**23 bottom** (© Shvaygert Ekaterina), **7 inset** (Nikolai Pozdeev), **15** (siamionau pavel), **17** (© Shvaygert Ekaterina).

Front cover photograph of a wheat field reproduced with permission of iStockPhoto (© Devon Stephens). Back cover photograph of a girl with a pile of T-shirts reproduced with permission of Shutterstock (siamionau pavel).

The publisher would like to thank Dee Reid, Diana Bentley, and Nancy Harris for their invaluable help with this book.

Every effort has been made to contact copyright holders of material reproduced in this book. Any omissions will be rectified in subsequent printings if notice is given to the publishers.

DUDLEY PUBLIC LIBRARIES
L
729412          Sch
        J633

# Contents

# What is a farm?

A farm is a place where food is grown.

pumpkin

Plants that grow on a farm are called crops.

# Plants for food

Wheat grows on a farm.

rice

Rice grows on a farm.

beans

Some farms grow vegetables.

Cabbages grow on a farm.

Potatoes grow on a farm.

Carrots grow on a farm.

**strawberry**

Some farms grow fruit.

Apples grow on a farm.

# Plants for clothes and fuel

Cotton grows on a farm.

Cotton is used to make clothes.

Rapeseed grows on a farm.

Rapeseed is used to make fuel
for cars.

# Planting crops

Most crops are planted in the spring.

The plants need water and sunshine
to grow.

# Picking crops

apples

The crops are picked in the autumn.

We can buy the food that has grown
on a farm.

# Can you remember?

What do plants need to grow?

Answer on page 24

# Picture glossary

**crop** plants grown on farms are called crops. Many crops are used for food.

**fuel** something we put into cars and lorries to make them go

# Index

Answer to quiz on page 22: Plants need water and sunshine to grow.

**Notes to parents and teachers**

**Before reading**

Ask the children if they have ever visited a farm. Ask them what plants they think grow on farms. Make a list together. What are these plants used for? Are they only for humans to eat?

**After reading**

- Read *The Little Red Hen* to the children. Talk about what the hen has to do to grow the wheat. Ask children to be the different characters in the story and 'hotseat' them, asking what that character thinks and feels at different points in the story.

- Show the children some cotton wool. Do they know where cotton grows? Show them on a map. What can they think of that is made from cotton? Then ask them what other materials we make clothes from. Do any of these materials start on a farm, too? Bring in some clothes made of cotton, wool, and linen for them to feel.